W9-BNO-962

Over 50
Most Commonly Used
Hawaiian
Words
and More
A Hawaiian Language Primer

✻ HOW TO PRONOUNCE THEM ✻
✻ WHAT THEY MEAN ✻
✻ WHEN TO USE THEM ✻

MUTUAL PUBLISHING

Jade Mapuana Riley

Dedicated to the Hawaiian People.
May we always remember that the
"Aloha Spirit" lies within us...

Library of Congress Catalog Card Number: 2003109323

Photos by Douglas Peebles
First Printing, October 2003
Second Printing, June 2004
2 3 4 5 6 7 8 9

Design by Mardee Domingo Melton

ISBN 1-56647-634-8

Mutual Publishing, LLC
1215 Center Street, Suite 210 • Honolulu, Hawai'i 96816
Ph: (808) 732-1709 • Fax: (808) 734-4094
www.mutualpublishing.com
e-mail: mutual@mutualpublishing.com
Printed in Taiwan

✳ INTRODUCTION ✳

This primer is for visitors and those new to the Hawaiian Islands.

The main purpose of this guide is to introduce you to the most commonly used Hawaiian words. Because many words have multiple meanings, this guide provides pronunciation, definitions and explanations of how and when to use these common words in everyday conversation.

This is a very basic list with a simplified pronunciation guide. If you are interested in learning more about the Hawaiian language, I encourage you to reference Mary Kawena Pukui's Hawaiian-English dictionary.

✳ RULES ✳

1. There are no consonant clusters in the Hawaiian language.

2. Hawaiian words must always end with a vowel.

3. Hawaiian words must have at least one vowel.

4. An okina (') is a glottal stop — it is also considered a consonant, so only appears between vowels.

5. The kahako (¯) makes vowels longer, so it occurs only over vowels.

✳ HAWAIIAN ALPHABET ✳

The Hawaiian alphabet consists of thirteen letters: the five vowels and eight consonants, the consonants being: *h, k, l, m, n, p, w,* the eighth is the *okina* (') – its sound is the glottal stop that occurs between "oh-oh". The vowels have two sounds, stressed and unstressed, as follows:

a, as in water	**ā**, as in ah
e, as in wet	**ē**, as in hey
i, as in bit	**ī**, as in police
o, as in obey	**ō**, as in bow
u, as in pull	**ū**, as in spoon

Two vowel combinations usually merge as a *diphthong*, some examples being:

ou, as in soul   **ai**, like "i" in light
oi, as in loiter   **au**, like "ou" in out
ae, like "y" in my   **ao**, like "ow" in how
ei, as in veil

❋ PLURALIZE ❋

There is no "s" in the Hawaiian language; to pluralize a word, you would put *nā* before the word.

Example:
pua – flower   **maka** – eye   **ʻilio** – dog
nā pua – flowers   **nā maka** – eyes   **nā ʻilio** – dogs

There are other ways to pluralize, but this is the easiest for this pronunciation guide.

a hui hou
(ah who-ee ho)

MEANING:

Until meeting again; till later.

MOST COMMON USE:

See you later.

ʻae
(eye)

MEANING:
Yes; to consent or agree.

MOST COMMON USE:
Yes.

'āina

(eye-na)

MEANING:

Land or earth.

MOST COMMON USE:

Land.

akamai

(ah-ka-my)

MEANING:

Smart or clever.

MOST COMMON USE:

Smart.

aloha
(ah-low-ha)

MEANING:

Love, respect, as well as hello or goodbye.

MOST COMMON USE:

A greeting, hello or goodbye.

'a 'ole
(ah-oh-lay)

MEANING:
No, not, never.

MOST COMMON USE:
No.

auē, or *auwē*
(ah-way)

MEANING:

Oh Dear! Whoops! Oh No!

MOST COMMON USE:

Oh Shucks! Whoops!

hale
(ha-lay)

MEANING:

House or building.

MOST COMMON USE:

House.

hana hou
(ha-na ho)

MEANING:

To repeat, encore, do it again.

MOST COMMON USE:

To do it again, encore.

haole

(how-lay)

MEANING:

Caucasian, white person, any foreigner.

MOST COMMON USE:

White person.

hele

(hey-lay)

MEANING:

Go, walking, going.

MOST COMMON USE:

Go; going.

hele mai
(hey-lay my)

MEANING:
Come.

MOST COMMON USE:
Come.

holoholo
(ho-low-ho-low)

MEANING:
To go for a walk or ride for pleasure.

MOST COMMON USE:
Going cruising.

huhū
(who-who)

MEANING:

Angry, offended.

MOST COMMON USE:

Angry.

huli

(who-lee)

MEANING:

To turn; to curl over.

MOST COMMON USE:

To turn; turn over.

imu

(ee-moo)

MEANING:

Underground oven; food wrapped
and cooked underground.

MOST COMMON USE:

Underground oven.

kai

(ky)

(KY as in SKY)

MEANING:

The sea.

MOST COMMON USE:

The sea.

kama'āina
(ka-ma-eye-na)

MEANING:

Native born person; host.

MOST COMMON USE:

The locals or islanders.

kāne
(ka-nay)

MEANING:

Male, man, husband.

MOST COMMON USE:

Male or man.

kapu
(ka-pooh)

MEANING:

Prohibited, taboo, forbidden.

MOST COMMON USE:

Forbidden or off limits.

keiki
(kay-kee)

MEANING:

Child, offspring, a kid.

MOST COMMON USE:

Child or kid.

kumu

(koo-moo)

MEANING:
Teacher; source.

MOST COMMON USE:
Teacher.

lani
(la-nee)

MEANING:

Sky, the heavens; heavenly.

MOST COMMON USE:

The heavens or heavenly.

lei

(lay)

MEANING:

Lei, garland. Necklace of flowers, shells, feathers, and all sorts of things. Usually a symbol of affection.

MOST COMMON USE:

Lei.

lōlō

(low-low)

MEANING:

Paralyzed, numb, or stupid.

MOST COMMON USE:

Stupid.

lū'au

(lou-ow)

(OW as in COW)

MEANING:

Young taro tops; also Hawaiian feast.

MOST COMMON USE:

Both. Depends on the conversation.
If you are talking about the Hawaiian feast
or dinner, then lū'au is used. When talking
about the taro plant, then lū'au leaf is used.

mahalo
(ma-ha-low)

MEANING:

Thank you. Also, admiration and respect.

MOST COMMON USE:

Thank you.

mahalo nui loa
(ma-ha-low new-we low-ah)

MEANING:

Big, large, or many thanks.

MOST COMMON USE:

Thank you very much.

maika'i
(my-ka-ee)

MEANING:

Good, fine, or excellent.

MOST COMMON USE:

Good or fine.

makai

(ma-ky)

(KY as in SKY)

MEANING:

Seaward, toward the sea.

MOST COMMON USE:

Toward the sea.

mālama pono
(ma-la-ma po-no)

MEANING:
Be careful, take care of; or to care for.

MOST COMMON USE:
Take care.

malihini

(ma-lee-hee-nee)

MEANING:

Stranger; visitor or tourist.

MOST COMMON USE:

Tourist or visitor.

mauka

(mow-ka)

(OW as in COW)

MEANING:
Inland; toward the mountains.

MOST COMMON USE:
Toward the mountains.

nani
(nah-knee)

MEANING:
Beautiful, pretty, splendid.

MOST COMMON USE:
Beautiful or pretty.

nīele

(nee-eh-lay)

MEANING:
Curious, inquisitive; a busybody
or nosy person.

MOST COMMON USE:
A nosy person.

nō ka ʻoi

(no ka oy)

(OY as in TOY)

MEANING:

Is the best.

MOST COMMON USE:

The best.

Maui nō ka ʻoi, Maui is the best.

nui
(new-ee)

MEANING:

Big, large, or many.

MOST COMMON USE:

Big or large.

ʻohana
(oh-ha-na)

MEANING:

Family.

MOST COMMON USE:

In referring to the whole family.

ʻono
(oh-no)

MEANING:

Delicious, tasty.

MOST COMMON USE:

Delicious, as in taste of food.

ʻōpala
(oh-pa-la)

MEANING:

Trash, garbage or rubbish.

MOST COMMON USE:

Trash or rubbish.

'ōpū
(oh-pooh)

MEANING:

Stomach or abdomen.

MOST COMMON USE:

Stomach.

pau
(pow)
(OW as in COW)

MEANING:

Finished, completed, done.

MOST COMMON USE:

Finished; all done.

Pehea ʻoe?

(Pay-hay-ya oy)?

(OY as in TOY)

MEANING:

How are you?

MOST COMMON USE:

In asking, How are you?

pilikia
(pee-lee-kee-ah)

MEANING:

Trouble of any kind, great or small.

MOST COMMON USE:

Trouble.

pohō
(po-ho)

MEANING:

Loss, damage; out of luck.

MOST COMMON USE:

Loss; as in something wasted.

poi
(p-oy)
(OY as in TOY)

MEANING:

Poi. Made from cooked taro and water.

MOST COMMON USE:

Poi. It is our starch, as potatoes
or rice may be for other cultures.

pua
(pooh-ah)

MEANING:

Flower or blossom.

MOST COMMON USE:

Flower.

puka
(pooh-ka)

MEANING:

Hole (perforation), opening.

MOST COMMON USE:

A hole.

pupule
(pooh-pooh-lay)

MEANING:

Crazy; insane.

MOST COMMON USE:

Crazy.

ukana

(oo-ka-na)

(OO as in MOO)

MEANING:

Baggage or luggage.

MOST COMMON USE:

Baggage.

wahine
(wa-hee-nay)

MEANING:
Lady, woman, wife.

MOST COMMON USE:
Lady or woman.

*Be aware! Some restroom doors are marked,
"KĀNE" or "WAHINE" in Hawai'i.

❋ PLACE NAMES ❋
(As you go around the island)

Waikīkī	.. Spouting Water	**Honolulu**	. Protected Bay
Wahiawā	. Place of Noise	**Haleʻiwa**	. House of the
Waimea	.. Reddish Water		Frigate Bird
Lāʻie	..... ʻie leaf	**Kawela**	... The Heat
Kahuku	.. The Projection	**Hauʻula**	.. Red *Hau* Tree
Punaluʻu	. Coral Dived For	**Kaʻaʻawa**	. The Wrasse Fish
Kahaluʻu	. The Diving Place	**Kāneʻohe**	. Bamboo
Kailua	... Two Seas		Husband
Pali	...... Cliff		

❋ STREET AND HIGHWAY NAMES ❋

Kamehameha .... The Lonely One

Lunalilo .... Very High (Sixth King)

Kalākaua .... The Day of Battle (Last King)

Liliʻuokalani ...... Smarting of the High-Born One
(Last Monarch)

Likelike............. (Princess)

Kaʻiulani .... The Royal Sacred Height (Princess)

Kalanianaʻole .... The Royal Chief Without Measure
(Prince Jonah Kūhiō Kalanianaʻole)

Kapi'olani .... The Arch [of] Heaven
(Queen; Kalākaua's wife)
Kapahulu .... The Worn Out Sail
Kūhiō .... Prince Jonah Kūhiō Kalaniana'ole
Ala Wai .... Fresh Water Way
Ala Moana .... Sea Road

✻ ISLANDS ✻

O'ahu .... Gathering Place
Hawai'i .... Big Island
Maui .... Valley Island
Kaua'i .... Garden Island
Lāna'i .... Pineapple Island
Moloka'i ...... Friendly Island
Ni'ihau .... Forbidden Island
Kaho'olawe

✻ DIRECTIONS ✻

Mauka .... Toward the mountains
Makai .... Toward the sea
Diamond Head ...... Toward Diamond Head
Ewa .... Toward Ewa (opposite direction
from Diamond Head)

❄ COUNTING TO TEN ❄

1 . . . . 'ekahi   6 . . . . 'eono
2 . . . . 'elua   7 . . . . 'ehiku
3 . . . . 'ekolu   8 . . . . 'ewalu
4 . . . . 'ehā   9 . . . . 'eiwa
5 . . . . 'elima   10 . . . . 'umi

❄ DAYS OF THE WEEK ❄

Pō'akahi . . . . Monday   Pō'alima . . . . Friday
Pō'alua . . . . . Tuesday   Pō'aono . . . . Saturday
Pō'akolu . . . Wednesday   Lāpule . . . . . Sunday
Pō'ahā . . . . . . Thursday

❄ MONTHS OF THE YEAR ❄

'Ianuali . . . . . January   Iulai . . . . July
Pepeluali . . . . February   'Aukake . . . . . August
Malaki . . . . . March   Kepakemapa . September
'Apelila . . . . . April   'Okakopa . . . October
Mei . . . . May   Nowemapa . . November
Iune . . . . June   Kēkēmapa . . . December

❋ PARTS OF THE BODY ❋

kino	body	ʻōpū	stomach
poʻo	head	wāwae	foot or leg
maka	eye	kuli	knee
papālina	cheek	lauoho	hair
waha	mouth	niho	tooth
poʻohiwi	shoulder	ihu	nose
poli	bosom	pepeiao	ear
lima	hand or arm		

❋ ʻOHANA (FAMILY MEMBERS) ❋

ʻohana	family
makua kāne	father, uncle
makuahine	mother, aunt
keiki	child
kupuna kāne	grandfather
kupuna wahine	grandmother
moʻopuna	grandchild
kaikuaʻana	older sibling/same sex
kaikaina	younger sibling/same sex
kaikuahine	sister of male
kaikunāne	brother of female
hiapo	oldest child in family
muli loa	youngest child in family
pōkiʻi	younger sibling of either sex